Praises for Breaking Chains

Oh my gosh! What a book! The story of this author's book definitely mirrors my life growing up as a child. The author's book has a virtually flawless pedagogy approach. She uses the book to help other women discover their inner beauty and to step outside of the walls that they find themselves in. Deborah Ware challenges other women to take control of their physical, mental, and spiritual health through regulating habits, resisting unhelpful comparisons, and embracing changes such as marriage and motherhood. She also opens up about her childhood, challenges with loved ones and her rough life of losing the battle of her children being turned against her by close relatives. Ware also reveals that she had been trying too hard to please everyone, by giving more love to people that she thought would love her back and trying too hard to make something work that didn't fit. She admonishes other beautiful, smart, intelligent women who might be going through trials or might have gone through similar situations to not do the same by making any single person their purpose for living. This book is filled with inspirational instances for women who feel stuck, not good enough, not beautiful enough, or not smart enough to walk into the path to realize their dreams and not limit themselves.

Minchen Toe

August|2019

OMG! Deborah Ware's book, "Breaking Chains" is a tear-jerker! I loved reading it and I am proud to have been apart of this project.

Belinda Robinson

August|2019

BREAKING CHAINS

BREAKING CHAINS

DEBORAH WARE

13TH & JOAN PUBLISHING

WWW.13THANDJOAN.COM

Breaking Chains. Copyright © 2019 by Deborah Ware. All rights reserved. No part of this publication may be reproduced, distributed, or transmitted in any form or by any means, including photocopying, recording, or other electronic or mechanical methods, without the prior written permission of the publisher, except in the case of brief quotations embodied in critical reviews and certain other noncommercial uses permitted by copyright law. For permission requests, write to the publisher, addressed "Attention: Permissions Coordinator," 500 N. Michigan Avenue, Suite #600, Chicago, IL 60611.

13th & Joan books may be purchased for educational, business or sales promotional use. For information, please email the Sales Department at sales@13thandjoan.com.

Printed in the U.S.A.

First Printing, October 2019

Library of Congress Cataloging-in-Publication Data has been applied for.

ISBN: 978-1-7331313-9-1

Dedication

I dedicate this book to my late grandmother, Ollie L. Gibson, for showing me how to be humble and loving to anyone that has wanted love, understanding, and the support of a family while giving all the love they have without reciprocation. I hope that my book will give any mother, father, daughter, son, wife, or husband the confidence to love themselves more and stop letting the misery of others block their blessings from God. I hope my story will teach them to hold no expectations because that will cause more misery. Writing this book broke the chains that were continuously keeping me feeling unworthy and unable to love myself. It was the closure that I needed. My biggest inspiration has also been one of the biggest blessings I've ever received: being married to a man that believes in me, protects me, and has remained by my side for 43 years of my life. He has been my supporter, protector, encourager, and the shoulder I needed to cry on during my most heartbreaking times. Without the support of my wonderful husband, I would not have had the strength or the belief in myself to share my story.

The Pursuit of Your Dreams Gives You The Power to Break Every Chain

-Deborah Ware-

Contents

CHAPTER 1: The Last Moments to Remember 9

CHAPTER 2: This is Who I Am 15

CHAPTER 3: The Early Years 19

CHAPTER 4: Where Do I Fit In? 27

CHAPTER 5: Darkness 31

CHAPTER 6: Too Much Credit 35

CHAPTER 7: Just A Dream 39

CHAPTER 8: My Prince Charming 43

CHAPTER 9: In and Out of My Life 47

CHAPTER 10: This is The Last Time 51

CHAPTER 11: Grandchildren 55

CHAPTER 12: False Hope 59

CHAPTER 13: Betrayal and Expectations 63

CHAPTER 14: My Hopes and Dreams 71

CHAPTER 15: Look At My Success 77

A Letter of Thanks to My Husband 81

Final Thoughts from the Author 83

About the Author 87

Foreword

Imagine growing up never really feeling total **LOVE**, never having heard the words...

"You're Going to Change the World".

At a young age Deborah never really felt like she was much! Every now and then her Mom and Dad would pour a little encouragement into her, but then drain it all up with anger and lies! Having to choose between the RESPECT of your mother and LOVE of your dad is a choice a child should never have to make. Helping others, with a kind word or act of encouragement has always been a part of Deborah's character. Having a musician for a father wasn't easy. The long rehearsals, days away from her friends and other family was hard for her, but her father knew what he was crafting... a soul singing diva! Growing up in Louisiana, a place enriched with culture and music, Deborah was destined for greatness. She always knew that there was more for her in this world and that she was going to do whatever it would take to get it!

What you are about to read WILL CHANGE your LIFE! It will cause you to rethink your communications with your friends, family and loved ones! When God gave you to your parents, HE made them promise to do the best they can always and if for any reason they can't fulfill that promise, HE will step in and help. Parents need only ask for his help! Deborah has faced rejection at every turn! She has heard **"You're never going to make it big"** from family members and even **"You're too old to be singing"**.

In this book you will hear how Deborah at every turn had to deal with hurt and heartbreak, and losing her father. He also revels a secret to prepare her for what comes next. She shares heartbreak such as having her own mother turn her kids against her, her sister turning her back on her, and a consistency of having her world rocked back and fourth like a ship without a sail.

There were times that Deborah was forced to keep the secrets of her father's intimate affairs from her mother, and eventually discovering the strength and courage to tell her mom. She was later told by her mother that she was HATED for it! Deborah wanted her father to understand but he became upset with her and treated her differently. It was only on his death bed that he reminded her that he still loved her!

After losing her father, her mother becomes a different person, who ignores her, talks about her to other family members, and even goes as far as to pit her own kids against her, while attempting to keep her down. Through all of this God had her back.

You see a long time ago, somebody prayed for Deborah. They prayed that God would order her steps and carry her though the fire when it came after her. In this book you see how despite all the odds stacked against her, she continues to fight, not with her fist, but with her music, affirmations and encouraging messages.

On this journey Deborah finds the Love of her life "John" and gives birth to three boys! She travels overseas and tackles music abroad. She has even met some musical legends along the way. From the outside it looks as if she has it all, but if you start to peel back the layers and see all the scars that she has from years/decades of attacks from family, friends and sometimes even people she has never met, you will understand how she lives and breathes positivity. When all you get is **BETTER**, it makes you achieve your absolute **BEST**, and allows you to appreciate every waking moment and every time your head touches the pillow at night. You learn to look up and tell God "Thank you."

Being **BEAUTIFUL** is about more than just your looks, it's about your style, your smile, your contributions to others, how you give back to the universe even when its not kind to you. Being beautiful is about how you respond when family, friends and others try and bring you down, and how you turn that into positive energy, that you pour back into others. Deborah chose to become an educator, and she has turned all the years of pain, hurt and frustrations into teaching the next generation how to do the same! This page turner will test you in ways you can't imagine! Deborah tells you the story of a little girl looking for the leadership of her father and compassion of her mother, while growing up with music on her heart.

Down the road Deborah embarks on a HUGE defining moment, the creation of **Live In The Divas Den**, a platform for independent artists to tell their story. Since starting this next chapter in Deborah's life, she has sat at the table with a lot of different people, from poets, to singers and songwriters and even everyday folks like you and me!

Later, Deborah added a co-host Andre Oliver (aka Andre Tyrone), providing a male's point of view and the rest is history! What does the future hold for Deborah? Well it's simple...to continue her mission to spread sunshine and happiness to all who need it.

So, Imagine growing up never really feeling total **LOVE,** never having heard the words

"You're Going to Change the World" **but with every single step you take, that's exactly what you're doing!**

Preface

Love is life and, as I was once told, life should be all about living to the fullest extent. I imagined life as being beautiful, spiritual, enjoyable, memorable, and filled with positive, healthy thoughts. Of course this was my thinking when I was younger, but as I grew up, I realized that my life was not at all that way. I'm certain that life is not a picture that's painted perfect for everyone, but I was so attached to the foolish fantasy in my younger years. But soon enough, that memorable part of my life took a detour and began to become surrounded by negativity that changed all the beauty, enjoyment, spirituality, and positivity about it. The beauty became painful because of the misery that was starving for company. I loved so hard for my family and friends that I totally forgot about loving and caring for myself. But despite all the adversity I've gone through, I have learned to let go and receive what God has given me and hold no expectations that will cause misery in my life.

CHAPTER 1: The Last Moments to Remember

There are certain moments in your life that you want to cherish forever, and there are some moments that are better left in the past. Breaking a chain is like breaking a curse or bad seed that continues to be planted. I remember the day I finally realized that there were many chains that needed to be broken in my life. When the day is already at an end, one moment of sadness can devastate you. The day that I am referring to is the day I wiped a row of tears from my father's eyes as he lay on a hospital bed in ICU, counting down the moments he had left of his life. Believe me when I say this was one of the most awful moments of my life. I had to see the sorrow, pain, and loneliness in my father's eyes. I will never forget the tone of my father's voice or the somber mood in the room. Hopelessness was printed all across my father's face. The silence began to grow in the room, and the glaring of my father's eyes became more and more glazed over. He stared at me as if to let me know that there was something he wanted to say, but he just couldn't find a way to say it. You see, my father was never the kind of man to say the words, "I love you" verbally.

As I stood by the side of the bed holding his hand, my husband captured a moment that he felt was going to be my last moment with my father, and he felt that it needed to be remembered. To this day, I look at that picture with sadness in my heart. Sometimes when I feel the brokenness in my heart, I turn and look at it and think to myself, If I only had one more day to express my love to you. Immediately after my husband captured that moment, my life started to take a turn that I will never forget. It gave me the purpose for writing this book.

The more silence filled the room, the more cold and somber the room seemed to get. My father's raspy tone cut through the silence as he asked me to wipe the tears from his eyes. My heart got so heavy. It felt like the adrenaline on a roller coaster as it drops. I remember feeling very warm and nervous as I proceeded to do as he asked. I tried hard to hold back the tears that suddenly began to fall down my face. I felt like he needed me to let go. This was the moment that I never wanted to experience or accept. He gazed all around the room without saying a word and then finally took a deep breath. He told me that things in my life were going to change and that I would begin to learn the truth about those that were closest to me in my family. He finally stated that he hoped that I would be able to deal with it all. My father seemed to have been holding on to this for a long time. You know, it's all becoming clear to me: my parents' relationship, me and my mother's relationship, all the ill feelings that my only sister had for me, the separation that my family would bring between my sons, and my father's will to stop holding on. All these things comprised of the many links in the chain of grief in my life.

My father passing was really a shocker to me and definitely changed my life. I can recall his final dialysis treatment the week before his passing. He was being very uncooperative with the nurse, looking up and down and around with a stare, almost a final look of despair. I remember consoling him, asking him to cooperate and be kind to the nurse. He turned slowly with a stare and said "okay" in a voice so small he could've been mistaken for a child. That day he wasn't doing well at all. Little did I know, the worst was yet to come. Not long after, he was sent directly to the hospital to be admitted.

My father loved going to the casino to play the One-Armed Bandit, so to take his mind off the reality that he was never going to get better, my husband tried to humor him by telling him that he needed to get better quickly so that he could go and have some fun. He told us that he wasn't worried about having fun. He was tired of the dialysis and tired of being treated badly. I could tell the frustration was setting in. This is when I realized that he was losing the fight to stay alive. This definitely was the end, and his words weighed heavy on my heart.

My family has been torn apart for five years since he transitioned into heaven. My mother began to treat me the same way my father was treated. She cut every tie with me as a daughter and turned those that I loved against me with no remorse. I began to lose all hope, confidence, and sense of self worth because I was told that I was nothing but a disappointment and that I did nothing to help the family. My dreams of having a loving, caring, and supportive family was deteriorating. To this day, I continue to live with no closure for all of the turmoil that ensued after my father's death. I've never gotten any answers, and I've been left to break these chains of sorrow and fight this never ending battle on my own. I still struggle, but each day I pray and develop a closer relationship with God. I continue to fall but I always get back up.

CHAPTER 2: This is Who I Am

I felt so phenomenal in my life because I raised my sons that are now grown and on their own. I laid the foundation down for them, however, after years of being a wonderful mother and role model, they have turned on me. All my effort was a waste of time. Once the betrayal set in, it made me feel like I did nothing but made their lives miserable. This thought is so heartbreaking, when I placed my hopes and dreams on hold to give my all to them. But no matter what they say about me, I know in my heart that I gave them my all.

I am many things: dreamer, inspirer, mother, grandmother, wife, and wonderful person to know. I am a phenomenal woman that is beautiful inside and out. For years, I had such low self-esteem and confidence, I didn't even believe in myself. It's true that words can hurt and make you see yourself and life in a bleak and hopeless way. I was known as the "ugly daughter" that was not mentioned. I was known as the stupid one who surmised things. However, today all that has changed. I refuse to give into those negative lies about me. I know who I am, and I know that I am worthy. Each morning I wake, I ask God for forgiveness and to protect me, my husband, our marriage, my children, and my grandchildren. I also ask Him to forgive and bless all those who are not comfortable with me being who I am. I never thought that loving others and caring about them would lead them to hate you enough to hurt you, but that is the sad reality of life. My daily regimen to remind myself that I'm worthy is looking into the mirror and asserting that I am an extraordinary person who feels outstanding in my own world. Only love, peace, and happiness will exist in my world. I will not allow regrets or loneliness to take over my world because I'm strong, I'm wise, and I'm such a phenomenal woman.

CHAPTER 3: The Early Years

"Love should never come with the price of being beat."

Cinderella was always one of my favorite fairy tale characters. She was a simple girl with dreams and goals that no one listened to or supported. When thinking of this fairy tale, it's easy for me to draw a comparison with my life. She was beautiful, but Cinderella had a very low self-esteem, and little confidence. Despite her pleasant demeanor, a clear difference shown between her and the two stepsisters she lived with: Cinderella was treated unfairly.

Every responsibility was placed on her shoulders, while her sisters lived a lazy and spoiled life.

Upon reflection, I can clearly see my life as an exact replica of Cinderella's. As the oldest in the family, I felt loved up to the age of

10, which is about the time in your life when you begin to mature and understand change. As the oldest, my family took every opportunity to blame any misfortune on me, and at that time in my life, I just always agreed with everything and accepted it as my sad reality. I guess when you just want to be loved, you will accept any way you are treated. I was treated differently, unfairly, and I was misled by my mother and father, which severely lowered my self-esteem. My confidence was torn all the way down. I often wondered when I would ever really belong.

This cycle of toxicity continued into my growth to womanhood. I was placed in the middle of my parents' entangled and dysfunctional relationship. It was like being torn between two cities. It's hard to thrive when your parents cannot give you consistent, stable love. I taught myself what real love was. And I accepted the fact that what little love I did get was the best it was going to get. It's almost funny how my family life was like a painted picture up to age 10. I can clearly remember the best photo taken by my father during Christmas, when my sister and I were the best of friends (or at least it seemed that way) .We were a family: my mother and father smiling, all of us together in our living room, all dressed up. That Christmas, we had a tree full of gifts; you know, the ice box, stove, dolls, and more. It seemed like such a happy time. We were happy. What ever happened to these memories, the smiles, the laughter, the happiness between my parents? It all seemed to abruptly end.

After these moments, I started to wonder about my parents love for me because their relationship as husband and wife started to change.

My father was no longer the perfect dad that I remembered on that Christmas morning when I was 10. You see, my father was a very attractive man, and other women definitely noticed. Obviously, this caused a lot of friction in the household. But friction turn to an explosion when my father committed adultery and began to live a double life. This was the part of my life when I became a pawn in my parents' relationship .My parents used me to play against each other, instructing me not to tell one parent what the other was doing. This was totally unfair, and it wasn't easy for me to keep harmful secrets as a child without feeling guilt inside, even though I really didn't know much. I never understood why or how my father could cheat on my mother, but fear kept me from asking any questions. I could not figure out why he needed to love someone else besides my mother—she was attractive and educated! My father was a well educated man, but he just didn't play his cards right. He wanted to have his cake, and eat it too. But there was an unseen reason for that as well.

There were times that I felt like a ball being bounced from one side of a room to another. One of my parents was always upset with me because I spilled the beans on the other. It was impossible to please everyone. All I knew was that I didn't like seeing my mother hurt, both physically and mentally, and that my father's actions were not acceptable. The most terrible thing about all of this was that my parents never saw eye to eye, and things got violent when I couldn't keep secrets from my mother. Telling my mother that my father was being unfaithful meant her confronting my father, and the dysfunction took center stage. My father didn't feel that he was wrong at all. In fact, he even went so far as bringing me in the company of his lady friends, telling me that they were related to me to cover his tracks. How was I supposed to know the truth at this young age?

These days were filled with my parents arguing and fighting, but I never understood why no one left. It got so bad. I can remember hiding various objects around the house, so my father couldn't use them to hurt my mother. Whenever these disagreements occurred, I was always the one to clean up the mess in the end. If my mother was crying because she was hurt, I was the one there to wipe her tears and encourage her to not worry. I would cry with her and tell her that everything was going to be alright, even though I knew it wasn't.

I was a protective daughter and placed my mother on a pedestal. I loved her so much—I could never imagine that she would turn on me. Her whole demeanor toward me changed the moment my dad passed. From this, I learned that one should not love or trust anyone too much. After my dad was gone, I became the daughter that never did anything for her, the daughter that disappointed her, and the daughter that didn't deserve to be noticed as my mother told me. It's heartbreaking to find out on social media that you are your mother's least favorite daughter. What did I do to deserve this kind of treatment? As the oldest daughter, I continued to love both my mother and father no matter how wrong they might have been. I just didn't know that the older I grew, the worse things would play out between them, no matter how much I prayed. God would still hear my prayer, but it was up to my parents to make a change.

The more I protected my mom, the more distant the relationship between my father and I got. Every time I would run and tell my mom the things I knew about my father, he trusted me less and less. He always called me stupid and said things like, "You are just like your mom...Get out of my face" and "Don't ask me for nothing." There was a time when I was in high school and I decided to enter the yearbook pageant. My parents were on bad terms at the time. I raised money for the pageant by selling cake that my mother baked for me. Out of hatred for my mother, my father took the money away from me the day before it was to be turned in. This was such a disappointment for me, and he didn't even care. The funny thing about this was that my father taught at the same high school I attended, and no one even knew what happened. I continued to cover things up and act as if I were living the perfect life. I continued to love my parents still, but they never reciprocated. My parents never verbally expressed their love for me or each other. That just didn't happen in the house that I lived in. My parents both had hearts that were cold as ice. The older I got, the more the dysfunction, fighting, vulgar language, and abuse grew. I can remember finding my mom in a pool of blood after a fight with my dad. I didn't have a driver's license, but I took her to the hospital. I hoped that she would begin to see that she needed to make a change in her life, but she continued to live with my father and take the abuse instead. I never understood why she felt she had to continue living under these conditions when she was an independent woman. I know now that no woman should be treated like this by a man that says they love them. However, this revelation was still a long way off. But what I did know was that I was living in a world that I would have to release myself from one day.

As I got into my teenage years, the dysfunction began to be revealed to everyone, including friends and neighbors. It was so embarrassing, but it didn't matter to my father. My mother tried to hide her bruises and scars by covering them up with makeup, but sometimes that didn't work. Her friends and coworkers began to see. Things got so bad that my mother's co-workers were alerted to ban my dad from coming to her job. My mother never told me anything good about my dad; she always told me how he was no good, but she continued to stay with him. In the end, she stated that her reason for staying was because she was caught-up. All in all, it still wasn't enough to make her move on with her life away from my father. As I look back on all of this dysfunction, I understand how abused and battered women today feel, along with how afraid and confused their children must be. It's unfair to put children through all of this turmoil, and then continue to stay in the end!

CHAPTER 4: Where Do I Fit In?

My mother never talked much about her family to me, no more than to say that her dad never took care of them and left her mother and sister when she was young. I could also hear the resentment in her voice when she recalled a time when her mother took a trip to California and did not take her. Apparently, her mom made this decision because she could not afford to pay for three tickets, so only her sister was able to go. This anecdote showed an obvious parallel to the difference my mom made between my sister and I. I was treated as less-than exactly like my mom. It wasn't fair to me! My mother only had one sister that lived a great life with four kids and a husband that owned his own business. My mom's relationship with her sister is the very same chain that links me and my own sister's dysfunction. The worst part is that no one will own up to—or even acknowledge—the resentment between all of us. We rarely visited my cousins and aunt, and my mother always asserted that we shouldn't visit because neither did they. My mom stayed standoffish until finally reaching out when my aunt was diagnosed with cancer. I never understood the reason for this tit-for-tat, however, now I recognize that this was part of the chain that I needed to break.

There were times that my maternal grandmother would visit, but it was only when my parents were not on good terms. My father would complain and be cold and unwelcoming toward my grandmother. He was not the kind of person who you could voice your opinion to without him becoming defensive and angry. My father even put my grandmother out of our house on multiple occasions just for her mildly irritating him! I knew that this was not right, but I was so afraid of my father, so I just cried. There was a constant atmosphere of animosity between everyone in the family. This was a sad time for me, as we never visited our cousins because the adults never got along. When your family is dysfunctional, you never know what you might see or hear during the course of the day. I felt like I was constantly on eggshells, bracing for the moment of impact at every turn.

As I became an adult, it all became clear to me that I needed to break this vicious cycle. All my life, I lived in negativity and selfishness, but I was determined to set myself free. I knew that to do this, I'd have to break the chain when I had a family...Little did I know how hard it was going to be to break it.

CHAPTER 5: Darkness

Living in a world surrounded by darkness can be extremely detrimental. I often wonder how many more individuals around the world are feeling this way. It's truly crippling. As I went through high school, I felt as though I lived in a cage with a lock that continuously prevented me from moving forward in my life. Living in the darkness felt like death to me. I felt as though I was only living in my parents' world. I felt this way because I lived only to hear my parents issues with each other about money, adultery, and more. There were times that I felt like I was being deprived of sleep, happiness, and a life that I deserved. My parents' problems became mental for me; they started to become mine. By this, I mean my mind was fed negativity, resentment, and hate. My mother carried around hate for my father for years, and my father carried around resentment for me. That really hurt and caused a lot of brokenness in me. I lived a very stressful and nervous life, which affected my way of thinking in school. Imagine living in an environment where no one ever agrees with each other, everyone is always in total competition with each other, and they treat you negatively when they are upset with each other. I was living in total HELL! I had nowhere to run and nowhere to hide, so I remained in the middle! It was time for me to think about how I would get out of this stressful situation. I knew it would be difficult. For one thing, I wasn't on my own yet, had no job, and no money. All I could do was dream and hope for peace. Seeing the light of day had to come soon just to end some of the pain that I witnessed in my home with my family. I needed to free myself from all the misery that I was living in. Freeing myself wasn't as easy as I thought, but I knew it was necessary.

CHAPTER 6: Too Much Credit

Sometimes we're guilty of loving too hard. I know we all say that we can never give out too much love, but we can when we run out of love for ourselves. Love should never have a price tag, nor should love ever be taken for granted. Family love should never be measured as being too high or too low. As both a mother and a daughter, I loved my family unconditionally. I never fathomed that one day I would wake up and the family members who I believed could do no wrong would turn their backs on me and not care less whether I lived or died. I know it sounds unbelievable, but I am living proof of the countless years of mistreatment. For years I said yes to every favor, offered help unconditionally, and gave certain family members more credit than they could ever deserve. If I had to do it all over again, I would certainly do it differently. I would love myself more than I loved everyone else.

For many years, I felt as though I wasn't good enough and didn't have enough to offer. I had such low self-esteem, I felt that I needed their love and approval just to feel special. When your self-esteem takes such a steep dive, you can fall into a deep depression where you feel that the world only revolves around that group of family members. I was once told that I should never expect anything from any family member, as they are always going to be the ones to hurt you. There were times that I would visit my mother and sister and felt like I didn't belong in their world because I wasn't just like them. I guess that's why my father told me that I would learn the truth about my family members after he passed. My personality, my demeanor, my perception of things was totally different than theirs. I never was the daughter with the perfectly shaped body, built to receive compliments and suit every man. I was the plain girl with a personality of her own. I really didn't care because I knew deep down in my heart that it wasn't what was on the outside of me that mattered to anyone that truly cared about me—it was my big heart that should be valued most. I used to get made fun of because of how skinny I was, how large my chest was, how plain I dressed, and how timid I was. I was always ridiculed and treated differently by my mother, father, and sister. The only solace I can remember was my Aunt Eloise who would stick up for me and tell them to leave me alone when I visited her. What is now very clear to me is that my parents rode the fence with my sister and I when they were upset with one another. I guess during those times, that was the thing to do: choose your kids to relieve your selfishness.

My dad never seemed to show very much love toward me from the time I was 10 years old. He felt that he could not trust me because he knew that my mother repeatedly told me that he was no good. As the oldest, I felt that it was my duty to report whenever I saw my father doing something my mother wouldn't agree with. The bad part about this was that once I told my mother, she would totally lie to me and say she would not tell him but did anyway out of her own selfishness. Struggling with the regret for upsetting my dad, and the obligation to tell my mom was entirely too much to handle. It was more difficult to deal with each time this would happen, and my Dad felt he could never trust me. My father would take his anger out on me and sling hideous insults at me. But even with all that, I still loved him.

I never understood why any of this was happening. Why did my mom choose me to tell all the negative things about my Dad ? Why not my sister? When I left home, I saw my sister grow and speak her mind, letting my mom know that she didn't want to hear any of the negative things about my father. At the same time, she would side with my father. I'm so glad that I have been freed from the prison that my life used to be. Leaving home was the best decision I could have ever made in my life to start trying to break a chain that had been weighing down my family from generation to generation.

CHAPTER 7: Just A Dream

Dreams are a series of thoughts, images, and sensations occurring in someone's mind while they sleep. Dreams are also cherished aspirations and ambitions. However, for me, what anyone would normally call a bad dream was the reality of my life. The events that have taken place in my life have been unbelievably shocking and hurtful. I have always been in denial about my family, especially when listening to others talk about being betrayed by those they love. I always thought that my family would never fit into that category, but I was surely wrong. I really think that I was just naive to everything and always felt family would be the last to hurt me, deceive me, and walk away from me. I've learned to never say what someone will not do. I loved my family unconditionally and would have given my all to them, but it's obvious they did not feel the same.

I've learned that family should be close, stay close, and refrain from causing hurt or betrayal to one another. Why would they want to hurt me? What did I do to deserve the hurt and betrayal that they have shown toward me? You see, I was always the one in the family to place my needs and wants on the back burner just to please others, so I would always say yes to everything. I always changed my thoughts and what I planned to do fit others and satisfy them. I was the one that tried to stay positive and keep my family together. I was also the one to let others talk down to me and treat me negatively for the sake of keeping the peace. However, I finally realized what I was doing to myself, burying all of my pain and true emotion for people who didn't even care. I learned a lot about my family members that changed my way of thinking. After no communication from my mother or sister for 6 years, my children began to change on me. Instead of asking me why things were the way they were, they began blaming me for the distance between other relatives. This was totally unfair to me, but they were so used to seeing me be the problem solver in the family that it made sense...until this became a cancer in the family. No one ever took the time to think about my feelings or my hurt. They just wanted me to make things appear happy for them. I came to the reality that they hated me. What is so sad is that after mothers raise their children, the children inevitably change. And the more you try to keep them from falling into the dysfunctional chains in the family, the more others try to make them believe that they're the peacemaker and their mother is actually the problem. It makes life seem so unfair. I've never felt so hurt in my life, especially because I never expected this. I always found time to do things for my children. I tried to take them and their families on outings and tried to speak with them continuously. Sometimes people are so unsatisfied with themselves that they see nothing but evil from those that have taken care of them their whole life.

I don't totally understand the reason for all the pain being thrown on me, which continues to add more links to the chain that looped everyone in this misery and took over the entire family. I have never been given the opportunity to defend myself. I loved my mother and always thought she loved me, but through these 6 years of no communication on her part and conversing with others on social media about me, I have learned that I was only living in denial. My husband spoke with my mother and asked her when was the last time she told me that she loved me ...and her reply was that she didn't know. However, at her age, she uses social media to bash me and let me know that I am not one of her favorite girls. She has always had hate in her heart for me, but she just didn't expose it to me until my dad died. Have you ever experienced someone hating you by association? Well, this is how my mother is about my father. She hated my father, so she hated me too. I believed in her and I just don't understand all of this. As the lyrics to my song "Just A Dream" say, Why did they treat me this way? I don't deserve this. I was always there for all of them. I never wronged them, but I guess they all felt that I just wasn't good enough.

CHAPTER 8: My Prince Charming

It was a warm, bright, and beautiful day when I met my Prince Charming. I can clearly remember that September day in New Orleans when I was walking the halls of my high school and saw, God sent me an angel, my wonderful husband of 43 years and counting. I was in the 9th grade, and he was my first serious boyfriend at the time. I feel that God brought him into my life for my salvation and to help me clearly imagine a life away from my parents' issues. In the beginning, our life wasn't a bed of roses; we had our ups and downs, we disconnected and separated from each other as any young teenage couple would do. We didn't truly understand each other and made foolish mistakes. My husband was raised in a single-family home with no father, and he had the impression that I was living the life of Riley. As it has been said, look past the outside to know the real deal and don't assume. As it turned out, my husband was the knight in shining armour that rescued me and began my journey of breaking the chains of pain.

We were married one year after graduation, and I had my first child in 1977. I was happy that I would now have the opportunity to be the parent that I wanted my parents to be. I was free and able to start living my life with my husband and child. The road was rocky, and there were times that I felt I needed my parents, but I knew that I wanted to live my life differently from them, so I dealt with my issues myself. I wanted what my parents didn't have. When you've lived in dysfunction for so long, you crave something different. Leaving home and starting a family of my own was the best thing I could have done for myself. It gave me the opportunity to build my confidence, while being independent. I truly believe that if I had not left home, I would have relived my parents' life of negativity and dysfunction. I wanted to experience a pure and authentic relationship, so having my first son gave me someone to love, hold, and nurture. It gave me purpose.

As life went on, my husband joined the army in 1979 to give my son and I a better life and stability, so we packed up what little we had and moved to Texas. I truly began learning what kind of woman, wife, and mother I was once I was removed from the mayhem at home. Don't get me wrong, things were tough and I still needed financial help from my parents. They gave me the support, but with stipulations behind it. I appreciated the help, but I knew it was given with resentment. Despite this, the chains were really starting to break for me. Finally, I wasn't in the middle of my parents' chaotic home anymore.

CHAPTER 9: In and Out of My Life

Sometimes life can feel like an open door. It can seem as if it keeps opening to the negative and closing to the positive. People come and go in your life. Those with all the wisdom, love, and sincerity leave, while those that only want to bring you misery, chaos, and pain remain. Sometimes family members are the ones that can never stay consistent. And the ones that try to be consistent transition into the heavenly place unexpectedly and leave you feeling lonely, helpless, and worthless. Why do I say this? Well, my life has been this way since the death of my Grandmother Ollie and my mother-in-law, Julia Carter. These two women were inspirational to me. They spent time with me, and they listened to me when I needed someone to understand what I was going through. They didn't ridicule me or try to destroy me by spreading horrible rumors about me. They never tried to place a divided line between my children and I, and they never sided with my children against me to hurt me. These strong, godly women believed that families should stick together. Reading a scripture from the Bible was their solution to any unsolved problem, not fighting, cursing, or betraying one another. For the last 6 years, I have been so lonely without them to comfort me from the drama I have dealt with.

For the last 6 years, my heart has been like a revolving door. I am a very broken, beautiful woman. I opened my heart to share my love, and my family took advantage of me. I can't seem to decide if their love for me was real as my love was for them. They have not spoken to me, visited me, or found me worthy of anything except for a text from time to time. I have never been so humiliated in all my life to see my family literally slander me on social media, especially when they don't realize that even though they blocked me and created ghost pages, outsiders were bringing the truth to my attention. Why? Why would family members stoop so low to tear someone down? Love is supposed to be real. God showed us all how to love and cherish those that are a part of our lives. So why is it so hard to show me the same love and care?

Growing up, I was a kid that just wanted to be loved. I never expected to grow up and experience family coming in and out of my life at their convenience, treating me as if I was worthless. I always acknowledged and recognized their accomplishments, but they never did the same for me. Mother's Days, birthdays, anniversaries, achievements at my job, and furthering my education have all been unrecognizable. There were so many inconsistencies in feelings of love among family that I often felt like I didn't belong. It really hurt me to feel this way about members of the family that I had great respect and so much love in my heart for. There were times when

I felt mistreated by my father, and I would ask my mother why, hoping that she would tell me something to ease the pain or clarify any misconceptions. Instead of comforting me, she compared the way he treated her to the way he treated me. She just told me not to worry about it. I was always uneasy and felt like he didn't have love for me. My father never took the time to say, "Daughter, I love you." Instead, he treated me the same way he treated my mother. However, I still forgave him and pretended in my head that he loved me in his own way. There was one occasion that my husband asked my father when the last time he told me that he loved me, and his reply was, "She knows I love her." Even on his transition to heaven, Dad still did not tell me he loved me. Instead, he told me that I was going to learn who my mother really was. It's been 6 years that my Dad has been deceased, and for 6 years I have been treated like hell by my family. I have almost suffered a stroke from the stress, and I've thought twice about going far out of everyone's way for good. I never understood what I did to deserve this treatment, and I began to accept it as my unfortunate reality.

CHAPTER 10: This is The Last Time

Pain, depression, and loneliness are feelings that we tend to encounter from those we love and care for. It has been said that your loved ones are the people that will place these feelings upon you. I've never claimed to be perfect, as we all have our flaws, but I asked for forgiveness while learning never to do it again. I have never set out to hurt anyone intentionally. Sometimes, these feelings bring you to a point of stress and exhaustion in your life. Suddenly, you begin to ask yourself those heartfelt questions that give you a feeling of depression and a desire to extract yourself from it all. After years of stress and my stroke scare, God got my attention, and acceptance of all those feelings of negativity I was experiencing really brought reality into my life.

This is my reality. I am able to still be here to tell you that the person that was forced to this reality and became closer to God was ME. Not to say that I was not in communication with God before, but

I just didn't fully allow him to use his power to help me. I always asked, "Why me," and prayed to God with an expectant ear awaiting an answer immediately. But I was impatient and I never released it to him 100 percent, giving him the opportunity to answer my call. I wanted to present my troubles to him, and still be my own hero at the same time. That was not happening! In other words, I didn't give it to Him , and walk away with confidence that He had this. Instead, I continued to spend my days and nights surrounded by negativity and misery.

As quoted in my song "This is The Last Time," All I would do is roll up and cry and ask myself, "Why do I always end up being wrong when I am the one that you can depend on and call?" I am and have always been overly concerned with everyone's feelings over my own. I was the one reaching out, trying to inspire and find solutions to their problems, and encouraging everyone to be better. I never considered that they didn't want to be inspired or cared about. They wanted to continue to be surrounded by negativity, drown in their own sorrows, and create more misery for themselves. I wanted to see them happy, peaceful, and positive, but they didn't have the same desires for themselves. According to my original song "This is A Dream," I tried, I tried, but at some point I had to move on from all this misery and make it better for me.

As a result of me trying and trying, I continued to hurt while being treated like I was unworthy of any positive treatment. I became a disappointment to some, being unable to help them (when I did everything that I could). I was also being separated from little loved ones that always fulfilled my life when the big ones tore me down. No matter what I did or no matter what I ever said, I was always gonna be wrong…I had so many pains hidden deep inside that, again, the way I dealt with it was that all I would do is roll up and just cry, as quoted in the lyrics "This is The Last Time". The chaos in my life was spiraling out of control, so when God got my attention, I listened. He told me that this was my life and I had to make an important decision if I wanted to live happily, peacefully, and prosperously. I had been given a second chance from God (and my cardiologist) so the ball was in my court.

Finally, I decided that as quoted in the lyrics of my original song, "This is the Last Time," With every pain it made me stronger, and I'm not going to waste it, so this is the last time that anyone would hurt me again. And this was the last time you close the door on me. Ultimately, I forgive my family for all that they have done to me. I have to live up to the King that created me and taught me that when negativity tries to fight against positivity, positivity has to win and prove that all the negativity is only a distraction that we let in ourselves.

CHAPTER 11: Grandchildren

I've been a mother, teacher, and singer, among other things. But one of the most precious roles I've been in is being a grandmother. Visions of going to the park and pushing my grandkids on the swing and merry-go-round was my dream of becoming a grandmother. I never really thought that I actually would be a grandmother as soon as it came to reality. Dreaming is one thing, but actually having it take place was a surprise. I can admit that I wished upon a star and prayed to God that one day I would have children of my own that I could nurture and be a great and caring mother to. Everyone has their own imagination of what it would be like to be a grandparent, and for me, my thoughts were that grandchildren were for the older generation that wanted a lot of kids. The first time I learned that I was going to be a grandmother, I felt that my sons were too young! They still had so many things in life that they needed to accomplish before creating a family. But, I began to think back to my days of becoming a mother, and I realized that I was being a bit selfish. If having children was what they wanted, and they felt ready to take care of them, I had no say-so in their decisions. One thing that I never did was suggest that they turn their backs on their responsibilities, children, or their children's mothers. I've always instilled in my sons that if they make a commitment to do something, and they were grown enough to start the commitment, then they must go through with it. Responsibility is a serious part of life, and I taught my sons that they must always take responsibility for everything they do. God created men and women to continue to grow his families and love them.

Well, I remember my first grandchild I laid my eyes on was a beautiful baby girl with light brown eyes that just made me never want to take my eyes off of her. She was a bundle of joy, full of laughter with juicy cheeks, and—yes— lovable! My outlook on being a grandmother was definitely changed, but there was one problem: the closer I tried to get to her, the more my family pulled her away from me. I felt like I was always being monitored around her, like I wasn't good enough. They made me feel like I couldn't be trusted with her. Why? I had no clue. This was my first grandchild, and my heart was so overjoyed to welcome her to a family that would always love her. So, I couldn't understand why there was always a coldness toward me spending time with her. I should have expected this, because I was not even invited to my first son's wedding where two families should have been joined together to welcome a new life into the world. I was hurt to the core, and wondered why I was left out. I gave my son nothing but love, attention, and care. We were so close, and I was always present for everything he took part in. I was a model parent to him. My children always came first in my life. In our home, we practiced caring and loving each other. Somehow after my kids grew up, all this changed. Mother became the enemy and unworthy of being present in their life. This was the point where I felt that becoming a grandmother was not like I thought.

From this point on, I tried my best to bring some positivity into the family. I failed at this, and the more I tried to connect the family, and surround my grandchildren with a loving family, the harder it got. The negativity continued. It's true that if things start out on a negative path, they will continue on a negative path, and one person can't fix it alone. I was hurt and had no support from other family to help make it better. On the morning of the wedding, I received a phone call from my father asking if I heard that my son was getting married. I was shocked and replied, "No, I did not know anything about this." Oh my, imagine how devastating it was as a mother for me to learn that the son I trusted and loved would do something like this. I felt betrayed and lost all hope. Why would someone that came from a family with great values fall to such a low point to treat their parents who did everything for them in this way?

When grandchildren become a part of the family, the child is supposed to gain two sets of grandparents, and the love of the child should be shared equally. I understand that life is not supposed to be perfect, but when you are raised in a family with good morals and values, this should not happen. This was a chain of negativity starting, and I knew it would have to be broken to prevent it from continuing on to yet another generation.

CHAPTER 12: False Hope

Everyone hopes to have two loving, caring parents that they can live a peaceful and calm life with. Knowing and experiencing love from your parents means a lot. After many years of learning that I was never wanted, I began to realize that all the feelings that my mom portrayed to me were not real at all. The love you get from your parents starts from before you even enter this world, but as you get older, things start to change. I never heard my parents verbally express their love for one another, nor do I ever recall hearing them express their love for me. It seemed that the words "I love you" were never spoken in our house, nor were the gestures of a kiss, hug, or sharing of happy moments ever shown. Remember, children learn to love from their examples given in the home. As I was growing up, I never saw those moments, so I had to learn to love as I got older. Sad to say, but that was the way of life for me. Each day was filled with hatred, brutality, and selfishness. Even if I was lucky to have a day that started with a positive moment, it would inevitably shift to negativity. I never knew what kind of day it was going to be in our home. All I could do was pray. Children should only experience happy times with their parents because they did not ask to be brought into this type of life. They should not be exposed to sorrow, brutality, and verbal abuse. I was more familiar with abusive vocabulary than positive vocabulary. These situations can have terrible lasting psychological effects on young children in a home. I had very low self-esteem as a child and this plagued me well into my adulthood. I always knew myself as "the stupid one". You know, if you hear something enough times, you begin to believe it. As I became a woman and had kids of my own, I learned how devastating this was to me. This destroyed me and my character to the point that whenever someone gave me a compliment, I felt that it wasn't genuine and that they were just feeling sorry for me. There were nights I didn't sleep because I was afraid that I would wake up and my mother would be dead or gone. I loved her and believed in her. When parents exhibit behaviors of brutality and verbal abuse around their children, they are being selfish. They should settle their differences away from the children and seek marital counseling, instead of continuing to make each other unhappy.

My parents didn't care enough about one another enough to try and save the relationship (no matter how strained) they had. All I ever prayed for was for a positive connection between the two to be made. Instead, I continued to go to bed each night with a nervous stomach, biting my nails until they bled. Despite the constant reminder that the love between them was dead and gone, I continued praying and praying while asking God to save me. I never gave up hope. I only made a promise to myself that as soon as I was old enough, I would leave and free myself from the misery that surrounded me. I vowed that when I had children, I would never expose them to this curse that I lived in. As Cinderella would do each day, I would do as I was told and continue to be isolated on the outside until I was rescued. My mother never seemed like she wanted to be rescued from her misery. To this day, she continues to be bitter and drown in her own misery, blaming me for everything to ease her pain. I continued to be thrown in the middle of my parents' turmoil until I was finally freed and began a life of my own without looking back.

CHAPTER 13: Betrayal and Expectations

It's true that when we are born into the world, we are clueless about life. Everything appears hazy and confusing, while every sound heard is loud, unfamiliar, and strange. We have no clue about wanting, expecting, and hoping for things such as love, affection, happiness, and the warmth of family. Yet, at this point of our new arrival, our born day, do we know what it means to have someone turn their backs on us? No, but we all experience this soon enough. As children grow, they begin desiring many things, including love and support from their families. As an educator, my job gives me a snapshot of loving children suffering without family support. Sometimes, they are not even fortunate to have parents. My heart aches for them. I loved both my mother and father dearly. Neither of them could do wrong in my eyes. But, in truth, I was just masking the wrongness that I saw.

I was one of those kids that deeply wanted the love, affection, and warmth from my parents, but because their relationship was in such a negative state, and the way their lives were before starting a family, I truly believed that it was just not possible to show they loved me the way I wanted and expected them to. Growing up, I had many things that I wanted in life, but the biggest thing I wanted was love from my parents. I wanted and needed their sincere love, not irrelevant material things.

Love is so important for the development of a child. Children strive for attention and love from their parents. That can be hard if their parents are living in two separate households, and the child is pressured to stifle their emotions because of the way the parents may feel toward each other. No, I didn't demand attention from my parents. As a matter of fact, I never even brought it to my parents' direct attention until I was 40 years old. I was not comfortable enough to bring it to their attention because my father was very strict. I just reduced it to the old saying that some things are better left unsaid. I continued to keep my suffering a total secret, remaining miserable and unhappy. I learned quickly that having expectations only got me involved in arguments where I'd be blamed totally for everything and expected to be the one to apologize. I waited for my family to realize the err of their ways and give me an apology, but I never received one. All I could do was cry from the frustration I felt. I guess I knew that having expectations wouldn't make a difference. From this, I learned that it is better not to expect anything from others, especially family, if you want to be happy.

I reached out and made attempts to open the door for my mother to come back into my life, but because she refuses to accept her responsibility in the six-year lapse in our relationship, nothing has changed. As I got older, I expected my mother and sister to show their love for me, but the more I expected, the more pain I endured. I never wanted this to happen. I went out of my way to please them just so my expectations would be met. There were times that I felt as though I was sucking up to them just to be loved. If I only knew what I know right now, I could have avoided a lifetime of sorrow.

If I realized how harmful expectations could be, I would not have been so easily hurt by my children when they betrayed me. I was blindsided when they cast me aside. It's funny, when I lived in Germany, far away from my family, raising my children was wonderful. There was no interference from my toxic family to hinder me from being the absolute best mother I could be. But all that changed when I came back to the United States. When I needed advice on how to guide my sons as they grew into manhood, my mother wasn't there to support me. All of a sudden, I became an outsider to my oldest and middle child, while their grandmother became their mother .The closer I got back to my family, the more the negativity started to set in. My children were older now, and I couldn't hide the ugly truth from them anymore. The secrets of dysfunction began to slip through the cracks and make their way to my children. They became consumed with it. The more I tried to block it from them, the deeper they sunk into the chaos. I became the crazy one. I became the one that wanted to keep the family separated. I became the enemy to my children, and a wedge was put between us. They didn't call. They didn't visit. I was told that I was a bad grandmother. My grandchildren were kept from me. The love given to them began to turn into hate for me as a parent, and I began to feel unworthy as their mother. I expected my children to follow in my footsteps and have a big heart like me, but they succumbed to the gloom of my family.

My family loves confrontation. They are not themselves if they are not arguing with each other. Well, I don't like confrontation at all, so I choose to avoid it and stay away. Anytime there is confrontation, ugly words are thrown around and someone leaves with hurt feelings. I felt very hurt and betrayed when my sister told me that I was the cause of my parents' rocky marriage. This was really hurtful because we lived in the same house and experienced the same dysfunctional living, but she thinks I was the catalyst for all of our misfortune. It's just ridiculous. But, when someone is operating out of hate, these are the things that fill their minds. My mother tainted my sister's mind by rehashing old disagreements instead of trying to adjust the problem by taking responsibility for her part.

Sometimes we don't think about what we say in the heat of the moment, and we get involved in situations that have nothing to do with us. Everyone is grown and should be able to handle their own problems to prevent misunderstandings about situations that take place miles and miles away from us. It's really a matter of minding our own business. I have been married to my husband for 43 years, and he has never had any altercations with my mother. As a matter of fact, he has been there for her when no one else was. As a result of my mother's inability to model the positive traits of a matriarch in the family, and perpetuating the negative chains of dysfunction between my sister and I, she decided to share her first unpleasant encounter that she had with my husband with my sister. My sister went way too far, slamming my husband with the most heart wrenching words. Sisters are supposed to be close and have an unbreakable bond. Instead, she was looking for something that she could use to hit me below the belt that would destroy me forever. Why would she do something as low as this to her own sister? The only reason that I can think of is that she truly hates me. I've never done anything to hurt her and have always loved her. Did she have proof of what was said? Of course not. She only had hopes that a marriage of 43 years would be dissolved and finally I would be just as miserable as her. Well, tough luck because me and my husband are stronger than that.

Remember, I am a queen made by a king known as God. My husband loves me. We were not a perfect couple that never split before, or ever had problems, but we love each other and we're committed to each other. Please don't judge me. Only God can do this. What God builds no man can break apart, especially after 43 years of marriage. I choose not to go any further with this toxicity from all the hatred my family members carry for one another. It's sad; it makes my heart ache because I always loved my mother and my sister. They showed me that they have no love in their heart for me and really don't care if we have a relationship or not. They never wanted a relationship with me at all. I had to move on with my life after many nights of crying and asking myself what I did to deserve this sorrow. Because of my strong relationship with God, I forgave them and I still love them. I pray everyday that God will change their hearts for their own well being.

Sometimes we can hope for things, but the way life is set up, it doesn't mean that we will get all we hope for. I can truly say this, because I have been hoping for love and affection from my family for a long time, but I've yet to receive it. So the hate and chains continue to grow. But the difference is, now I refuse to subscribe to the drama. In times like this, we have to tell ourselves, "I can't do this anymore. I have to move on. I'll always love you, but I can't continue on into the misery." Sometimes we have to realize that things are too big for us to handle, and give it to God.

CHAPTER 14: My Hopes and Dreams

Playing dress up in my Granny's high heels, putting on lipstick, getting in the role of a teacher while playing school, and standing on my bed with my hairbrush microphone were the good days. These were the days when I dreamed of what I wanted to be when I grow up. I'm sure that we can all recall those times when we did these things as a kid. Growing up, I always had high hopes for myself. I dreamed of many things, but at this time, all I could do was imagine and role play. Little did I know, these were the things that I would pursue as an adult! It's funny! When you are a kid, it never dawns on you that you have to actually grow up in order to become what you wish to be in life.

I can recall dreaming of being happy, having a family with children, a husband, and a house with a white picket fence. When dreaming about being a mother, I had visions in my head of being showered with love from my children all the time. I hoped that they would always think that I was the best. Little did I know, that this would only remain a dream. I also envisioned celebrating my years of life and marriage. I never imagined worrying about when I will leave this earth or being a disappointment to my children. I dreamed of being the perfect mother, tucking my children in each night, singing sweet sounds to them. It was my purpose, above all, to protect them and keep them out of harm's way. I also dreamed about pursuing my love for singing and teaching. I can remember daydreaming about performing in bright lights on a stage. I never stopped dreaming, even when others laughed and had already written those dreams off for me. You see, as I was dreaming, God was listening and encouraging me to keep going. I can attest to that , because while I was dreaming and role playing, my father was creating a path for my dreams to start becoming a reality. Even though my father had a dark side in his life that I never condoned or agreed with, he was a constant provider in our home and never left his family. He was also very educated and was a talented musician. My father was a graduate of Grambling State University, and he had his master's degree from Loyola University in New Orleans. He was smart, gave some good advice, and even laughed sometimes. He always made sure that I was a participant in every sport, every talent competition, and was a well rounded dancer. I attended dance classes at Rosenwald Gym under the instructions of Mrs. Chapman. I even learned to roller skate there as well. Those were the good days that I remember. Although I was enrolled in all of these activities, as I got older, I began to see that just because I was enrolled in these activities, it didn't mean that my life was perfect; it was the happiness of living as a family that really mattered. Living in a drama-filled home with two resentful parents makes extracurricular activities seem so pointless.

I had very low self-esteem when I learned that people knew me as the "ugly daughter". Can you imagine how hurtful that was to me? I felt humiliated, and became more closed up, not wanting to speak out or participate as much when I got to high school for fear of how I looked and what people thought of me. By some miracle, I got past all of this anxiety and achieved my dream of becoming a majorette. My dream became a reality, and I became captain of the squad in my senior year.

Now that I am grown, and have raised my family, I see why my father did all of this: to keep me well rounded. However, as I reached my teenage years, he began taking all the activities I loved from me. I never dreamed of being a swimmer professionally, but if I had, I was well prepared for it. My father was a great swimmer. He was actually the first African American Instructor Trainer for the American Red Cross in New Orleans. I learned to swim at an early age and received many medals and awards for competing in different swimming meets. I trained to be a swimming instructor and a Water Safety Instructor that trained others to be lifeguards. My summer jobs always consisted of me working as a lifeguard. Today, I continue to be a great swimmer, and I hope to own another big house with a large pool in my backyard when I retire. I want to use my gift of swimming to teach others.

My biggest dream started when I was around thirteen years old. I loved to pretend and role play as a kid. I always loved music and singing. I was in the choir in elementary, middle, and high school. When my father learned that I had an interest in singing, he began doing what he could do to help me take it to the next level. Remember, my father was a very strict man and if he started something, he was going to work hard to finish it. Because I loved singing, my sister and I spent five days a week in the studio for vocal training. This was during the '70s, and we had the opportunity to work with other artists like Jean Knight who was known for her hit song, "Mr. Big Stuff" and with Stax Records and King Floyd for his single, "Groove Me" with Malaco Records. My father also formed a band called Black Acid to play behind us. The singers, "The Soul Emotions" consisted of my sister, Annie Mae Council, Sandra Anderson, Williemae Bridget, Donald White, and the late Eleanora Dodson. We traveled and performed every weekend at various venues. We performed cover songs and originals. This was fun some of the times. As long as my parents were getting along, things were good. But there were times that going to these gigs made me unhappy, because of my parents' fighting.

We consistently practiced, while keeping up our studies, but what I didn't like was not being able to have time to be with friends. However, I did not let this deter my dreams. I never thought that I would ever sing a song in a studio, but that dream unfolded and came to reality. My father wrote two songs: "It's Time for Love" and "Can You Feel," and we actually recorded our first 45 record on wax in Jackson, Mississippi at Malaco Studio. This definitely was a dream come true for me, because I was the lead singer on "It's Time for Love"! Now, let me tell you what made that dream so special. One day, as I sat in my high school homeroom waiting for the announcements, my father introduced our song to the entire student body! It was played over the PA system all through the school. Can you imagine this moment that I had dreamed about? I really felt like a celebrity. But it didn't stop there. We had interviews at the radio stations (WYLD and WBOK) and performed on television, and more. This made me realize that dreams can come true. Unfortunately, the dream seemed to be fading away because everyone decided that they no longer wanted to continue singing. This is when I moved on to my next dream of going to college, getting married, and raising a family. My love for singing never dissipated though, and I began teaching to pass along my passion for music. I soon learned that I could use my dream of singing to inspire and teach my sons, along with the students that I would be teaching. Remember, dreams only die if you let them and forget them.

CHAPTER 15: Look At My Success

Look at me. Look at how my life has changed. I have let go of the misery, gained a closer relationship with God, realized my worth, and finally started loving myself. Success is when one can say that they have accomplished what they've worked hard for and can now see the positive results as the effect of their hard work. After all the betrayal, hurt, and my dreams not being supported by family, my life is amazing! I feel so blessed! My life has definitely been tested, but my dreams continue, and are now the reality that has given me the closure I needed in my life. My life is beautiful, amazing, and couldn't be more satisfying. Throughout all of the changes my life has endured, I continued on with my education. I have earned my master's degree in Reading Literacy, an endorsement in Gifted Education, and currently an endorsement in ESOL. I have been awarded and commended for the success of my students on their State Standardized Assessments, and I continue to be an inspiration to the students that I have had the opportunity to teach. I no longer seek the love that I used to long for from my family. My heart has gotten lightened to everyone because of how they treated me. I don't rely on their love any more. I know my worth!

Everyday that I look into the eyes of my students and those that I work with, I smile because I can feel the love. I am so grateful for the friends that are there to comfort me when I need any reassurance of my worthiness. My confidence about what I love doing is so much stronger now that my strides have taken height. My love of my music has never been supported by all my family, and I used to feel defeated by it. But, I've done my best to stay consistent with showing my strong compassion for what I love: teaching, and singing. As a result of staying consistent, I have written, recorded, and released two complete albums and two singles. I've performed in coffee houses, appeared as an extra in movies ATL and We Are Marshalls, performed The National Anthem for the Atlanta Braves, Gwinnett Braves, and hockey teams. I've put out videos on Vevo and Youtube, I am the CEO and owner of my very own Indie talk show Live in The Divas Den. I started my first non-profit organization called Project Prom. And finally, I am the author of my first book about my life, dreams, and hopes called Breaking Chains.

I've learned many things during my life, but the most important thing that I've learned is to love myself first and know that I will always be worthy. Because of my relationship with God, I no longer need validation, because I am a queen made by a mighty king. I am a queen that can now sit on my own throne strongly, because I am just who I want to be. I am beautiful, and I will always be loved by God and my Prince Charming, John.

A Letter of Thanks to My Husband

Dear John,

I'm taking this moment to let you know how grateful I am for the encouragement and love that you have given to me through the process of writing my first book. You have been by my side, encouraging me to follow my dreams of telling my story. You have supported my dream from the first day I made the decision to make this book a reality. Your love and affection through the process has been the strength that I needed to fight off any negativity that tried to defeat me and take away my determination to complete what I dreamed of doing. The late nights that you stayed up with me were everything to me. My heart melted when you comforted me, when my stories brought tears to my eyes. You are an amazing man, and I have spent 43 years of my life with you. You are my right and left arm. You continue to keep me strong and determined to be better at everything that I attempt to do. I love you with all my heart and soul. God placed you in my life for a reason, and I couldn't be happier.

With all my love,

Debbie

Final Thoughts from the Author

After writing this book, I no longer feel that I am a burden or unworthy of love. I no longer feel broken. What I do feel is that I am more confident in myself, and who I truly am: a beautiful queen made by a mighty king. I'm blessed, I am grateful, and I am whole again.

Deborah Ware

"Beautiful"

B E A U T I FU L...spells Beautiful.

Nothing is more beautiful than you and me.

I am beautiful,

I am a queen on my own throne.

God made me just who I am, a ravishing queen with a heart of gold.

I am a goddess, can't you see? I am just who I want to be.

There is nothing more beautiful,

Than a queen like me because...

I am beautiful. I am beautiful in my own way. I am beautiful. I am beautiful.

There's no doubt how beautiful I feel.

I love being told that I'm beautiful. It makes me feel so good.

My most beautiful curve is my smile, and it drives me wild.

It's not hips, thighs, or my style; it's my confidence and my smile that drives me wild...

I am beautiful. I am beautiful, yes. I'm beautiful. There's no doubt how beautiful I feel.

I'm so beautiful in my own way.

You see, beauty is not only composed of the qualities found on the outside of us; it's not the way we look or how we dress. Instead, it's the way we humble ourselves. Beautiful doesn't mean that you are perfect. It means that you have the confidence to recognize that you are beautiful.

It's not my hips, thighs, or my style; it's my confidence in my smile because I'm beautiful. There's no doubt how beautiful I feel.

About the Author

13th & Joan Author Deborah Ware was born and raised in New Orleans, Louisiana . Deborah is the mother of three sons, grandparent of eight grandchildren and wife to retired Army Sergeant John Ware .Deborah is a 5th grade English Language Arts and Social Studies teacher in Gwinnett County in Georgia . Aside from teaching, and writing her first book, Deborah is a natural at creating stories through songwriting for the world's delight . Her gifts serve as encouragement and advocacy for discovering both inner and outer beauty . Writing and dreaming has also evolved as therapy for Deborah and she places great value on her ability to leverage her dreams to inspire those who struggle with self-confidence . Deborah's only wish is for every life that she touches to be inspired!

www.ingramcontent.com/pod-product-compliance
Lightning Source LLC
Chambersburg PA
CBHW021118080526
44587CB00010B/565